The DOG LOVERS'
Guides

German Shepherd

The **DOG LOVERS' Guides**

Beagle
Boxer
Bulldog
Cavalier King Charles Spaniel
Chihuahua
Cocker Spaniel
Dachshund
French Bulldog
German Shepherd
Golden Retriever
Labrador Retriever
Miniature Schnauzer
Poodle
Pug
Rottweiler
Siberian Husky
Shih Tzu
Yorkshire Terrier

German Shepherd

By Gill Ward and John Ward

Mason Crest
450 Parkway Drive, Suite D
Broomall, PA 19008
www.masoncrest.com

© 2018 by Mason Crest, an imprint of National Highlights, Inc.

Printed and bound in the United States of America.

Series ISBN: 978-1-4222-3848-6
Hardback ISBN: 978-1-4222-3856-1
EBook ISBN: 978-1-4222-7935-9

First printing
1 3 5 7 9 8 6 4 2

Cover photograph by Roman Milert/Dreamstime.com.

Library of Congress Cataloging-in-Publication Data is on file with the publisher.

QR Codes disclaimer:

You may gain access to certain third-party content ("Third-Party Sites") by scanning and using the QR Codes that appear in this publication (the "QR Codes"). We do not operate or control in any respect any information, products, or services on such Third-Party Sites linked to by us via the QR Codes included in this publication, and we assume no responsibility for any materials you may access using the QR Codes. Your use of the QR Codes may be subject to terms, limitations, or restrictions set forth in the applicable terms of use or otherwise established by the owners of the Third-Party Sites. Our linking to such Third-Party Sites via the QR Codes does not imply an endorsement or sponsorship of such Third-Party Sites, or the information, products, or services offered on or through the Third-Party Sites, nor does it imply an endorsement or sponsorship of this publication by the owners of such Third-Party Sites.

Contents

Key Icons to Look For

Sidebars: This boxed material within the main text allows readers to build knowledge, gain insights, explore possibilities, and broaden their perspectives by weaving together additional information to provide realistic and holistic perspectives.

Educational Videos: Readers can view videos by scanning our QR codes, providing them with additional educational content to supplement the text. Examples include news coverage, moments in history, speeches, iconic moments, and much more!

Series Glossary of Key Terms: This back-of-the-book glossary contains terminology used throughout this series. Words found here increase the reader's ability to read and comprehend higher-level books and articles in this field.

Chapter 1

Introducing the German Shepherd

The German Shepherd Dog is one of the most popular breeds around the world. His natural presence and noble good looks, coupled with his versatility as a working dog and loyal family companion, are the reasons why the breed is held in such high regard. No other breed is as effective in so many widely varying situations, living and working alongside people. German Shepherds are at work worldwide as police dogs, using their tracking and searching skills, and their courage defending their handlers, as well as apprehending and detaining criminals. The German Shepherd is also widely used by the armed services, because he is adaptable enough to cope with foreign postings.

The breed has distinguished itself as a search and rescue dog. The amazing scenting ability, sharp hearing, outstanding endurance, and the weather-resistant coat of the German Shepherd enables him to cope with extreme weather and environmental conditions, searching for avalanche, earthquake, and explosion victims. He has saved

many lives due to his determination in searching for human scent in appalling conditions.

The versatility of a German Shepherd's character, such as being calm, obedient and confident, has seen him in the role as a guide dog for the blind and as an assistance dog. German Shepherds have served us faithfully throughout history—this is a multi-talented dog and a truly unique breed.

Companion dogs

The German Shepherd is prized as a working dog, but the fact is that the majority of Shepherds are in pet homes, where they live stimulating and fulfilling lives. However, before you take on a German Shepherd, you must first decide whether you can meet his needs.

The German Shepherd is capable of great loyalty and devotion. He is alert and responsive to training, which he will need whether it is formal obedience or just for good manners. He is a fun dog who can show pure joy just messing around with his family. His lively enthusiasm requires guidance, not inhibiting, so as a prospective owner, you need to be calm, firm but fair, understanding, and consistent in your interactions with him. He will get along well with children as long as he is well socialized with sensible youngsters. He will give you companionship, affection, and a sense of security, as well as encouraging you to get plenty of exercise.

German Shepherds 101

German Shepherds are slow to mature, especially mentally, so puppy mischievousness may remain into adulthood. Your dog will need plenty of mental stimulation to keep his active mind from finding its own entertainment. This may include chewing the furniture, digging up the garden or barking—he can be very creative when trying to relieve his boredom.

German Shepherds are very motivated by movement, which is why toys and balls can be useful training aids, but this characteristic can become a problem. Moving objects, such as other dogs, joggers, or cars, may attract his attention and he could be tempted to chase. This is why early training is very important.

This is a breed that can be very demanding of your time and

budget. You will need to make sure that your yard is secure, which means fencing at least 5 feet (1.5 m) high, as a German Shepherd is very agile and can clear heights that other breeds of the same size may not consider jumping. You must also be aware of how much it will cost to keep a large dog such as a German Shepherd, and be sure you can afford to take on this responsibility.

The Shepherd's double waterproof coat will shed heavily, usually twice a year, but to some degree it can shed almost continuously. You must therefore be prepared to groom your dog regularly and buy a good-quality vacuum cleaner to minimize the amount of dog hair around the house.

German Shepherds can become over-attached to one person, so it is vital to recognize the huge commitment involved in socializing a puppy with a variety of people. It is also important that all the family is happy to have a German Shepherd and are willing to share in the daily care.

Developing the breed

There are hundreds of dog breeds and many have their roots in the very distant past. However, the German Shepherd is a relatively young breed, developed in Germany at the end of the 19th century.

Its story began as a herding dog, but through the vision of one man who developed the breed's mental and physical qualities, the German Shepherd found his place as a true partner to humans.

In rural Germany, farmers used a variety of herding dogs, and although the dogs shared similar characteristics—such as intelligence, strength, and endurance—they varied in appearance depending on the region. The sheepdogs working in the highlands and the hills were small, stocky, gray dogs with erect ears; the sheepdogs working on the plains were larger and more athletic, able to trot effortlessly all day on the flat terrain.

The first German Shepherd Dogs

Captain Max von Stephanitz is known as the father of the breed. In 1889, he saw a working yellow and gray shepherd dog at a dog show in Karlsruhe in western Germany. The dog looked like a wolf, and possessed stamina, power, intelligence and steadiness. Von Stephanitz bought the dog, renamed him Horand von Grafrath, and registered him as the first German Shepherd Dog.

He was impressed by the German Shepherd Dog's herding heritage, intelligence, work ability, and strength of character. He established the Verein für Schäferhunde (Society for the German Shepherd Dog) in April 1899. This was the first breed club for the German Shepherd Dog, and the SV continues to be the largest German Shepherd breed club in the world. A standard was developed that emphasized mental stability and utility. The captain's motto was, "Utility and intelligence." To him, a dog was worthless if he lacked the intelligence, temperament, and proper structure to make him a good working dog.

Von Stephanitz was also responsible for expanding the job description of German Shepherds to include messenger, rescue, sentry, and personal guard dogs. Their sheer physical strength and versatility, combined with their ability to work in bad weather and adjust to climate changes, made them excellent working dogs as well as outstanding companions. Soon they were being used by the police, and were entering civilian police dog trials with the help of the SV. In 1902 the SV published the first rules for police and service dog training.

In World War I, though, the full potential of the German Shepherd Dog became apparent. Daily tasks included carrying dispatches, which sometimes involved carrier pigeons attached to a body harness,

and assistance laying communications cables through trenches and across battlefields. Essential food supplies were carried between the trenches under enemy fire. These were just some of the courageous feats these dogs performed.

The American German Shepherd

The first German Shepherd was shown at a U.S. dog show in 1907, and the German Shepherd Dog Club of America was founded in 1913.

In 1917, when America entered World War I, all things German became "the enemy." The American Kennel Club (AKC) changed the name of the breed to the Shepherd Dog and the German Shepherd Dog Club of America became the Shepherd Dog Club of America. In the U.K., the name of the breed was changed to the Alsatian.

In 1931, the AKC restored the name to German Shepherd Dog. However, in the U.K., the breed was known as the Alsatian until 1974.

Soldiers returning home after World War I told tales of the wonderful dogs they had seen in action, and some even brought German Shepherd Dogs back with them. One such soldier was Lee Duncan, who imported a German Shepherd named Rinty. He saw the dog's remarkable potential and after specialized training, Rin Tin Tin became a movie star, and did much to popularize the breed.

Unfortunately, the breed paid a price for its sudden uptick in popularity. Unscrupulous breeders started producing puppies on a mass scale, with little regard to their soundness of temperament and conformation. It took many years for breeders to rebuild the breed.

During World War II, German Shepherds were hard at work on both sides as mine detectors, sentinels, guards, messengers, and at other tasks. In America, Dogs for Defense was formed, providing thousands of dogs to the military.

The breed suffered greatly in Germany, especially after the war, when food shortages meant many great dogs were destroyed. It wasn't until about 1949 that the breed recovered in its homeland.

The German Shepherd today

The modern German Shepherd has become one of the most versatile of all breeds. His striking appearance draws admiration in the show ring and his working ability is prized in a variety of disciplines.

He is the second most popular breed in the U.S. (by AKC registrations), and remains breed of choice for the police and security services, where his courage, loyalty, intelligence, and tracking skills are put to the test. He is highly valued as an assistance dog, and he competes with distinction in many of the canine sports. It is this combination of good looks, versatility, and outstanding companionship that makes the German Shepherd so very special.

Chapter 2

What Should a German Shepherd Look Like?

The breed standard is a written description of the ideal German Shepherd Dog, describing the physical aspects, temperament, and character of this legendary breed. It is used as a blueprint by breeders and judges so that only the very best dogs are used to produce future generations. Here we look at the main points of the breed standard.

General appearance

The German Shepherd Dog is an alert, well-balanced working dog. Ideally, she is of medium size and strong, with a well-muscled, powerful build. She is slightly longer than she is tall, and presents an outline of curves rather than angles. The sexes are clearly defined, and give an impression of masculinity or femininity.

Temperament

A German Shepherd should be direct and self-confident. She is highly intelligent and very active. The ideal German Shepherd is a calm, confident, and loyal dog, but she must also display courage and resilience in the defense of her owner and property. She should be friendly with her family, but observant and somewhat aloof with strangers. She should never be aggressive, nervous, or shy.

Head and skull

The German Shepherd's head should be noble and cleanly chiseled, with a keen, intelligent, composed expression. It should be in proportion to the body without being coarse, too fine, or over-long or pointy in the muzzle. The general appearance should be slightly broad between the ears. The forehead should be very slightly arched, with little, or at the most only a slight trace of center furrow when viewed from the front or side.

The muzzle should be long and strong, with tight lips. Its topline should be parallel to the topline of the skull. The eyes are medium-size and almond-shaped. They should not be round or protrude, and should be as dark as possible, giving a lively, intelligent and self-assured expression.

The ears should be firm in texture and broad at the base. They should be set high, almost parallel—not pulled inwards or tipped—tapering to a point, open at the front,

and should never give the impression of being soft or loose, which would cause them to hang forward or lean over sideways. They are carried erect when the dog is at attention, the ideal carriage being one in which the center lines of the ears, viewed from the front, are parallel to each other and perpendicular to the ground.

The jaws should be strongly developed with a perfect, regular and complete scissor bite (the upper teeth closely overlap the lower teeth and are set square to the jaws). The teeth should be healthy and strong, consisting of 20 in the upper jaw and 22 in the lower jaw.

Neck

The neck is strong, clean-cut with no skin folds, and relatively long. The muscles should be well-developed. It should be carried at a horizontal 45-degree angle, raised when excited, lowered at a fast trot.

Forequarters

The shoulder blades should be long and set sloping at a 45-degree angle, lying flat to the body. The upper arm is strong and well muscled, joining the shoulder blade at about a right angle. Both the upper arm and the shoulder blade are well muscled.

The forelegs are straight from the pasterns to the elbows when viewed from any angle, and the bone should be oval rather than round. The pasterns should be strong and springy, and slightly angulated. The length of the foreleg should slightly exceed the depth of the chest. The feet are short and compact, with well-arched toes, thick, pads, and firm, short, dark nails.

 Coat and Color

The German Shepherd should have a thick undercoat, and an outer coat consisting of straight, hard, close-lying hair that's as dense as possible. The outer coat is medium length; a slightly wavy outer coat, often of wiry texture, is permissible.

Colors can be all black; black saddle with tan, or gold to light gray markings; as well as all gray, with lighter or brown markings, known as sable. The undercoat is gray or fawn. Strong, rich colors are preferred.

Whites, albinos, blues and livers are not accepted within the breed standard, although puppies of these colors can be born occasionally and make perfectly fine companion dogs. The nose must be black in all colors.

Body

The withers (the point at the top of the shoulder) are higher than and sloping into the level back. The back is straight, very strongly developed, and relatively short. The breed standard says, "The whole structure of the body gives an impression of depth and solidity without bulkiness."

Breed guide

The chest is deep, and is carried well down between the legs. The ribs should be long and well formed without being barrel-shaped or too flat. The loin is relatively short, and the bottom line is only moderately tucked up in the loin. The abdomen should be firm, not paunchy.

Hindquarters

The hindquarters are the powerhouse of the dog. They should be strong, broad and well-muscled, enabling effortless forward propulsion. The breed standard says, "The whole assembly of the thigh, viewed from the side, is broad, with both upper and lower thigh well muscled, forming as nearly as possible a right angle. The upper thigh bone parallels the shoulder blade while the lower thigh bone parallels the upper arm." The hocks should be short, firm, and strong to give firmness and endurance in movement.

Tail

The tail should be bushy and reach at least to the top of the hocks, but not beyond the middle of the hock joint. When at rest, the tail should hang in a gentle saber-like curve; when moving, the tail will be raised, ideally never above the level of the back. When very excited or playing, the tail might be raised higher.

Movement

As a trotting dog, the movement follows a sequence of steps in a diagonal pattern, moving foreleg and opposite hind leg forward simultaneously. Well-balanced limbs and good proportions allow for an effortless, far-reaching gait. The German Shepherd is capable of maintaining this pace for long periods of time, which was required for her original function as a herding dog.

Parts of a German Shepherd

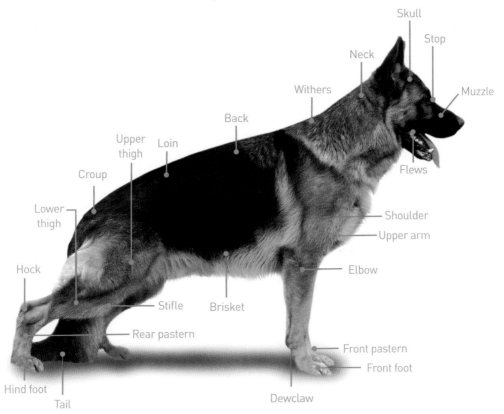

Size

The desired height for males at the top of the highest point of the shoulder blade is 24 to 26 inches (61 to 66 cm); and for bitches, 22 to 24 inches (56 to 61 cm). The German Shepherd is longer than tall, with the bred standard declaring that perfection is a proportion of 10 to 8.5. The length is measured from the point of the breastbone to the rear edge of the pelvis. The length comes not from a long back, but from the length of forequarters, withers, and hindquarters.

Summing up

It is important to bear in mind that the breed standard describes the perfect German Shepherd Dog. Breeders should aspire to produce dogs that conform as closely as possible to this written blueprint, because it describes the essential German Shepherd Dog.

The parts of the standard that describe structure are essential to the health and working ability of the dog. The parts that describe temperament are a big component of what makes a German Shepherd a German Shepherd. But a dog who does not meet the standard because her ears are not right or her tail is too short or her coat is the wrong color can still be a fabulous pet.

Chapter 3

What Do You Want from Your German Shepherd?

Over the many years that I've raised German Shepherds, I have met many people who have also chosen to share their lives with the breed. Most have found this partnership a deeply rewarding experience. But sadly, there have been a few owners who have made the wrong choice because a German Shepherd was not compatible with their lifestyle or experience.

Most German Shepherds who end up in an unsuitable home have been chosen by people who simply liked the look of the breed and had not considered the dog's behavior and activity level. Prior research to gain some general knowledge about the German Shepherd will help you decide if it is the breed for you, and will guide you toward selecting the puppy best suited to your lifestyle.

The German Shepherd is one of the most versatile of all breeds, and although he is the dog who can do it all, it will be in your best interests to decide exactly what you want from your dog.

Companion dog

If you want a Shepherd purely as a pet, you still want a healthy, good-looking representative of the breed, but you will not need to worry about the finer points that are required in a show dog. In terms of temperament, you should be looking for a more laid-back individual who does not have the strong drive of dogs bred specifically to work.

Working dog

Do you have ambitions to get involved in one of the canine sports, such as competitive obedience, tracking, agility, or Schutzhund?

If so, go to a breeder who has produced dogs specifically for the discipline you have in mind. This way, you stand the best chance of getting a dog who has the motiva-

Background on Shepherds

tion—and the ability—to compete at the highest level.

Taking on a Shepherd with working potential requires a lot of commitment from you, as this type of dog needs a great deal of mental stimulation. You will have to set time aside for his training—and not give up when the going gets tough or if you find something else to do. A German Shepherd has outstanding working potential, but he does need your time, your patience, and your guidance to get the best out of him.

Show dog

To help you make the best choice of puppy, study the breed standard and learn as much as possible about training a dog for showing. The best chance of owning a dog of show quality is to go to a breeder who specializes in breeding show dogs and has achieved a reputation for producing top-class dogs who are sound in both mind and body.

A reputable breeder will do their best to help select the right puppy. However, they cannot guarantee the puppy will be a successful show dog, as even a very promising puppy can change as he grows. For example, you cannot tell if an eight-week-old puppy will have missing adult teeth or if there will be a fault in the ear carriage—both of which would end his show career. However, this would not be a problem for a pet dog.

The parents' show record, health credentials, and breeding history should all be taken into account. And remember, a show puppy needs and deserves the same love, attention, and socializing as a pet puppy.

What your Shepherd wants from you

Every breed of dog has its own special needs, but the German Shepherd is one of the more demanding. This is a highly intelligent dog, built on athletic lines, with a lot of energy. He has a strong work ethic and will not thrive unless you, his owner, are willing to spend time training him, socializing him, and exercising him. This is true whether you own a show dog, a working dog or a companion.

Exercise

Most people are attracted to the German Shepherd for his intelligence, his good looks, and his temperament. Hopefully, you are also looking for a companion to keep you fit and active, because this is a breed that needs regular and varied exercise every day—regardless of the weather.

A quick walk along the streets on a leash with a run just on the weekend is not enough. He will need a mixture of energetic free-running in a safe, suitable area, games such as retrieving a ball or finding hidden toys, and exploring new places with you, such as woodlands, beaches, and the countryside.

The amount of exercise a German Shepherd requires will depend on his age and fitness. An adult will need at least an hour of interesting and energetic exercise a day. Do not think that leaving him out in the yard alone is adequate—apart from chasing the birds, he will probably just wander around at a snail's pace, sniffing as he goes. This will not provide sufficient exercise or mental stimulation; owner participation is definitely required!

On the other hand, it is vitally important that puppies are not over-exercised. Your pup may seem to have boundless energy, but

you need to bear in mind that his joints are still developing and his bones have not calcified. A growing puppy who is given strenuous exercise can do irreparable damage to his body.

Socialization

This is an ongoing process, but the most important work is done during the first 18 months of your Shepherd's life. For a dog to live in a family, and in the larger community, he must develop the confidence to cope with everything he comes across. This means he must take all situations in stride, reacting calmly in different and unfamiliar environments, and meeting people and other dogs without nervousness, apprehension, or aggression.

It is your job to educate and socialize your Shepherd by taking him out and about, so that he can get used to all the sights and sounds of the modern world. This is vital work, as your Shepherd needs to learn the social skills that will make him a model canine companion.

Training

Some owners assume that training a German Shepherd is only for people who want their dog to perform formal obedience in competitions. In fact, you can't live with a large, energetic, untrained dog.

Actually, training is part of building a close bond with your dog, as it is essentially a two-way communication process. It would be simple if dogs and people spoke the same language, but since dogs have their own life values and body language, it is important that you have an understanding of how dogs communicate and learn.

Using dog-friendly training methods in a consistent, clear, and fair manner is the key to successful training. Your training method affects not only your dog's behavior, but it can affect the dog's ability to learn in the future.

Whatever training you do with your German Shepherd, look on it as teamwork—developing a relationship based on trust and respect on both sides.

Other considerations

Before you start searching for a German Shepherd, you should narrow your choice so you know exactly what you are looking for.

Male or female?

A question I am often asked is: Will a male or a female make the better pet? The simple answer is that both males and females can be equally loyal family companions with the right socialization and training. That said, there are several important considerations that could determine your final choice of male or female.

The male is significantly larger and stronger and will be more likely to challenge you, especially during the adolescence phase, as he will experience an upsurge in the male hormone, testosterone. As an adult, he can be quite competitive, even aggressive, with other male dogs, but he usually gets along with females.

The female is smaller and usually less territorial. She is often more affectionate and easily trained, so perhaps easier to manage for the first-time owner or a family with young children. She will come into season (estrous) on average twice a year, for a period of three weeks. She may show behavioral changes during this time, associated with

the hormonal changes she is experiencing. This can range from being more affectionate to being a little sensitive or excitable.

To avoid an unwanted pregnancy, a female must be kept away from all male dogs during her season. Of course, she could be spayed (surgical removal of the ovaries and uterus). This will eliminate the inconvenience of the seasons and has a number of associated health benefits.

More than one?

If you already have a dog and you are planning to get a puppy, the general advice is to choose the opposite sex from the one you already have, as competition between the same sex can lead to friction later on. If you have a regular visitor to your home who brings a dog, follow the same advice of choosing the opposite sex. This will help the dogs to establish a harmonious relationship, especially when your puppy matures.

Unless you can keep them apart when the female comes into season, it would be wise to have one of them neutered. Aside from the risk of an unwanted litter, the male may go off his food, howl, urine-mark his territory (even in the house), or cause damage to the home in trying to reach the female if he picks up the scent of her in season. This is all natural behavior for an unneutered male. If the male is neutered (surgical removal of the testes), his instinctive desire to reproduce is removed.

Two together?

You may be tempted to take on two puppies at the same time—particularly if you see a litter of puppies and cannot make up your mind which one to choose. However, this is really not a good idea.

You may think rearing two puppies will be twice the fun, but in reality, it means twice the work. They will rely on each other, especially if they are from the same litter, and will naturally bond more closely together. This will make general training, and particularly bonding with you, very difficult.

A single puppy will learn to communicate and interact with his human family, which will make training easier and establish a much closer bond. Even if you bring a puppy into your home with an existing older dog, you need to remember that because humans and dogs

are different species, it is natural for the puppy to bond strongly with the other dog. They communicate in the same way and enjoy playing the same games. This could be to the exclusion of you.

If you decide you want two dogs, it is advisable to wait until the first dog has gone through the adolescence phase, has been well socialized, is under control, and you have formed a good relationship with him.

An adult dog?

Raising a puppy is time-consuming and hard work, so an older dog may be a better option for you. Sometimes you can get a an older puppy from a breeder, who has held onto him for a few extra months to see if he will turn into a good show prospect. This youngster may make a highly suitable pet, with only a minor cosmetic fault that would make him unsuitable for the show ring.

The other option is to take on a rescued dog who needs another chance of finding a loving, forever home.

The advantage of taking on an adult dog is you can assess his character and decide whether he is likely to fit into your lifestyle. The possible drawback is that the dog may have already formed some bad habits. You will need to find out as

Rescued Dogs

You may decide to take on a rescued German Shepherd, giving a dog another chance to find a loving, permanent home. Many breed clubs run rescue groups, and the big all-breed rescue charities are always looking for new and reliable owners.

There are many dogs who end up in rescue through no fault of their own – marital break-up, moving to a new home, or the arrival of a new baby are the most common reasons why dogs need to be rehomed. However, there may be some German Shepherd who have not received the training and socialization that is so important with this breed and, as a result, they may have some behavioral problems.

If you plan to adopt a rescued German Shepherd, find out as much as you can about the dog's background to make sure you can cope. It is no kindness to rehome a German Shepherd, only to hand him back because his behavior is too challenging for you.

much as you can about the dog's history and temperament, as well as his general social behavior. For example:

- Is he good with men and women, and children of all ages?
- Does he get along with other dogs?
- Will he coexist with any small animals you have at home as pets?
- How does he behave around the house?
- How does he behave in the car?
- What socializing has he had?
- Is he reliable and well-behaved on leash walks?

It can be immensely rewarding to rehome a dog, but it should not be undertaken lightly. In most cases, it is preferable if you have experience of owning dogs—and German Shepherds in particular—before you take on this challenge.

German Shepherd rescue groups always have adult dogs who need of new homes. If you decide on a rescued dog, make sure the organization is affiliated with a breed club or a reputable national organization. And make sure they will give you some post-adoption support, and will take the dog back if things do not work out.

Chapter 4

Finding Your Puppy

I f you have decided the German Shepherd is the breed for you, the next serious consideration must be finding a reputable breeder. Where should you get your puppy? There are a couple of options, but some are far better than others. Do not just buy the first puppy you see or hear about. Do a little homework first, and find a responsible breeder.

Many puppies are advertised on the Internet, and photos of German Shepherd puppies (or any breed, for that matter) will look adorable. But not every adorable puppy grows into a healthy, well-adjusted adult. The Internet is a good source of information, but the recommended sites are those run by national kennel clubs, where you will also find advice about choosing a puppy and finding a reputable breeder. However, just having a website does not make someone a responsible breeder.

Breed clubs may be able to put you in touch with local breeders. Recommendations from veterinarians, and people who have already

bought from a particular breeder are also usually reliable.

When looking for a German Shepherd, make sure you know what you want, how much you are willing to pay, and that you have researched the health and requirements of the breed.

Puppy farms

Puppy farms, also known as puppy mills, should be avoided at all costs. A puppy farm is a place where many puppies are bred and there are usually (but not always) many different breeds. The puppies are bred for financial gain, with little or no regard for the well-being of the mother or the puppies in the long term. Dogs in pet stores come from puppy farms—even if the pet store tells you the dog is from a breeder. They mean a puppy farm breeder, not a responsible breeder.

Do not buy a puppy because you feel sorry for her. You run the risk of taking on a sickly puppy who will cost you a fortune in vet bills, and may well end in heartbreak.

Responsible breeders

Responsible breeders raise their puppies at home and underfoot. They have one or, at the most, two litters at a time. They carefully study the pedigrees of the male and female before they arrange any breeding, with an eye toward breeding the healthiest, most temperamentally sound dogs. Responsible breeders belong to a breed club and are involved in their breed.

Responsible breeders register their puppies with a well-established registry such as the American Kennel Club or the United Kennel Club. (Registration with a well-established kennel club is a guarantee that your German Shepherd is truly a German Shepherd, but it is not a guarantee of good health or temperament.) They are able to hand over registration documents at the time of sale. Their breeding dogs are permanently identified by microchip or DNA. They screen them for hereditary health problems, and can tell you exactly which screening tests their dogs have had and what the results were.

Responsible breeders socialize all their puppies in a home environment. They provide written advice on feeding, on-going training,

socialization, parasite control, and vaccinations. They are available for phone calls after you buy their puppies, and will take a dog back at any time. They have a written contract of sale for each puppy that conforms to your state's laws.

They should also have lots and lots of questions for you. Don't be offended! They take seriously their responsibility for every puppy they produce, and that's a good thing.

Puppy watching

When you have found a breeder you are happy with and they feel you are a suitable owner, the all-important visit can be arranged.

For the first three weeks, the puppies do little but eat and sleep, so there will not be much to see. The mother will be closely bonded to her new babies and it is unfair to let strangers invade her privacy during these early weeks. Puppies are very vulnerable to disease, so most breeders will ask you not to visit after you have just been to another kennel, as infection can be transferred very easily.

The best time to view the puppies is at about six weeks old. By this time, they will be aware of their surroundings and their individual characters will be emerging.

When you first arrive, check the puppies' living conditions. They should be clean and smell fresh, with space to play and exercise, as well as a cozy bedding area. A healthy puppy will be lively. Her body

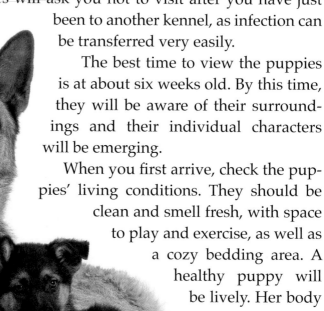

will feel firm and well covered, but the skin should feel loose. The coat and ears will be clean and the eyes bright. Check that there are no dewclaws on the hind legs; they are left on the front legs on German Shepherds.

Meeting the puppies' mother is very important, because her behavior has a big influence on her offspring. She should be happy and confident, although she may be a bit protective of her puppies. If she growls, backs away, or is aggressive, her puppies may have picked up the same traits, so it could be a risk taking one of them.

A reputable breeder will be happy to let you meet their adult dogs, which should be in good condition and greet you with wagging tails. If you watch how the breeder treats the dogs and how the dogs respond, it will give you an overall idea of how the puppies have been handled.

Choosing from the litter can be difficult, as all puppies are irresistible, but the breeder will help you find the puppy who is most likely to suit your lifestyle. A caring breeder spends so much time with the puppies, they will know the individual characteristics of each one.

Family companion

If you are choosing a pet, temperament is paramount. The puppies should be friendly, outgoing, and happy to be around you. If you have children, watch their interactions, as some pups seem to have a natural affinity for young children. A puppy who is wary or runs away and hides is not a good choice. A very domineering, pushy individual who objects to being handled is equally unsuitable. Both

these extremes need an experienced owner. An average puppy, who is neither over-demanding nor nervous, is most likely to make a well-balanced pet.

Working potential

You will be looking for a puppy who is confident and likes to play. She should be happy to approach you and curious if something new is introduced. She should be a natural retriever who likes to carry different objects and explore new environments. The puppy should be sociable and friendly, and interact positively with the breeder.

Avoid a puppy who is shy, will not follow you or play with you, or shows signs of being hyperactive. If possible, see the puppy on her own—as well as with her littermates—to check her responses.

German Shepherd puppies

Show potential

Puppies will change as they develop, but an eight-week-old puppy with show potential must have the right proportions and be well-balanced. She should move straight and sound when viewed from the front and behind. She should have a scissors bite.

The ears may have started to lift slightly at the base, which is a good indication that they will come up. (The ears flop about charmingly in puppies.) A fine skull or overlong muzzle in a puppy may not develop in the correct proportion to the body. For a show dog, a rich, thick black and gold coat is desirable.

Chapter 5

Getting Ready

Bringing your puppy home is an exciting time for you, but it can be unsettling for the puppy to cope with such an overwhelming change of circumstances. There are certain preparations you should make before getting your puppy, to help him settle in as smoothly and safely as possible.

In the yard

The yard must be securely fenced to a minimum height of 5 feet (1.5 m) to keep an adult German Shepherd in. The gate should have a lock and a sign asking people to make sure they shut the gate. Check that the fence and gate do not have any gaps the puppy might squeeze through or under. If the gate is left only slightly open, a puppy could wriggle through, with disastrous results.

A puppy investigates new objects with his mouth, so small stones could be swallowed, as most puppies seem to delight in picking them up.

Find out if your yard and garden contain plants that are poisonous to dogs. There is not enough room to list them all here, but you

can find a full list at www.aspca.org/pet-care/animal-poison-con-trol/toxic-and-non-toxic-plants.

Toxic chemicals, such as pesticides, motor oil, and antifreeze, need to be stored out of reach. Garden ponds seem to fascinate puppies, so if you have one, use a cover or protective fencing to make sure your puppy cannot accidentally fall in. If you have a swimming pool, make sure your puppy does not have access to it.

In the home

Your house will need the same safety inspection. Keep all detergents, cleaning chemicals and medicines stored well out of the puppy's reach. Ornaments and breakable items may need to be relocated. Houseplants at floor level will attract the puppy's attention. To stop him doing a bit of pruning, keep them—and anything else that could be a danger to the puppy—out of the way. Stairs can be very hazardous for a puppy. A baby gate at the bottom of the stairs or between rooms will restrict his access.

Cover or move electrical wires and keep children's toys out of reach. The puppy cannot discriminate between his chew toys and everything else.

You can provide a box full of safe toys for him to play with, but if there is a power cord to pull or a child's small toy tucked behind the sofa, you can be sure your puppy will find it.

Going shopping

Before bringing your puppy home, have an enjoyable shopping trip. You'll want these essential items on hand and ready for the new arrival.

Dog bed

Wicker baskets, beanbags, and wooden beds look attractive, but they are very chewable. The most practical type is the durable, rigid plastic bed, which is easy to wipe clean.

Make sure to buy a bed that is big enough for an adult German Shepherd. Line it with washable bedding, such as a fleece blanket or fleecy veterinary-type bedding.

Crate

A crate is a very useful piece of equipment that can be used both as sleeping quarters and also as a safe den when you cannot supervise your puppy.

Line the crate with fleece bedding and add a few safe toys, and when your puppy is feeling tired,

Crate training tips

put him in the crate with some treats. Do not shut the door; let him go in and out as he wishes.

When the puppy is comfortable going into the crate, close the door for a short period. To start with, make sure your puppy can see you when he is in the crate. Gradually, he will use it as somewhere he can relax and sleep safely, as dogs are den animals.

Please note that a crate should not be used as a form of punishment, and neither a puppy nor an adult dog should be confined for long periods, except for overnight.

Food

The breeder will tell you which food your puppy has been eating, so make sure you buy the same. Any change of diet must be done gradually to avoid stomach upsets.

Bowls

A food bowl and water bowl made of stainless steel are tough and easy to clean. Avoid plastic bowls, as these will be chewed. German Shepherds seem to like playing with their bowls, so a nonspill water bowl is a good idea.

Collar and leash

Puppies grow rapidly, so an adjustable, lightweight collar made of soft nylon is a good choice. As he grows, you can replace it with a fancy leather collar. Have an owner ID tag attached to your dog's collar, even if he is microchipped.

A light nylon leash will be fine for the first few weeks, but as the puppy grows, it becomes increasingly uncomfortable to hold. A good-quality leather leash is the best option.

Toys

All dogs, especially puppies, love toys. Providing your puppy with his own toys to play with and to chew is essential. There is a good selection available and choosing is fun, but remember that a

German Shepherd—even a puppy—has strong jaws. Check the toy to see that it is well made and does not have any small parts or pieces of fabric that could be chewed off and swallowed. Safe, durable toys include large knotted rope tuggers and natural rubber toys that are made for puppies to aid teething.

Grooming gear

The German Shepherd sheds heavily twice a year (called "blowing coat") at the change of seasons, and moderately year round. Keep-

Finding a Veterinarian

An important person in your dog's life will be your veterinarian. It is a good idea to do some homework before you bring your puppy home, so you can check out the facilities of veterinary practices in your area.

A vet who is knowledgeable about German Shepherds can be a real bonus, as she will be aware of health problems related to the breed. You may be a client of the practice for many years, so friendly and helpful veterinary staff, and a vet who takes the time to explain things and answer your questions, is essential.

ing his coat tidy will require regular grooming. You will need an undercoat rake-type comb, a metal comb, a slicker brush, and a bristle brush.

Settling in

When you first arrive home with your puppy, be careful not to overwhelm him. You and your family are hugely excited, but the puppy will be in a completely strange environment with new sounds, smells, and sights.

Some puppies are very confident, wanting to play right away and quickly making friends; others need a little longer. When you take your puppy indoors, let him investigate on his own. Show him where his bed is, which should be in a quiet, draft-free place, and show him his bowl. Fresh water should always be available.

Meeting the family

Help the puppy to establish good relationships with all family members through careful introductions. If you have children, do not let them chase the puppy, trying to make friends. Get them to sit quietly and let the puppy come to them. If they gently stroke him and give him a tasty treat, it will create a positive association right away. Remind the children not to pick the puppy up or encourage the puppy to play-bite them.

Children and puppies can be great friends if they are taught to respect each other. Supervise all interactions between them, because it is your responsibility to help develop a safe and happy relationship.

Give your puppy few days to settle in before you invite friends and relatives to see him, as all the attention can be too much for him and he will tire very quickly.

Introducing house pets

Introduce your puppy to the other house pets one at a time. Proceed carefully, because the initial meeting will leave a lasting impression. If you have another dog, make sure you do not change her usual exercise, attention, and feeding routine, as this may cause resentment.

Most adult dogs are very tolerant with puppies, but however trustworthy you think your dog is, the first introduction to the puppy must be controlled and well-supervised. Dogs can be possessive over their toys, food, and bed, so remove anything that could be a source of conflict.

Although it is important to protect the puppy, try not to interfere too much, as sorting out the hierarchy is essential to dogs (who are social animals). Do not leave them alone together until you are absolutely sure they are getting along.

Once your older dog has accepted the puppy, they should settle down and work out their relationship. Just make sure they both have time alone to rest and sleep undisturbed.

A German Shepherd will generally get along with the family cat. Introductions should be made with the puppy restrained—either by

being held or being put in his crate.

The cat must be able to move away from the puppy—preferably onto a higher surface—so that she does not feel trapped. Be careful, as a cornered cat may scratch the puppy and damage his eyes. By restraining the puppy when he first meets the cat, you can ensure that he doesn't discover how to make the cat run and the thrill of chasing her. Encourage the puppy to look at you for a treat or play with a toy instead of paying attention to the cat.

Feeding

Your puppy will be accustomed to eating with his littermates, so eating on his own could affect his appetite. He may eat less than the recommended amount or eat the whole thing as fast as possible, as he is used to competing with his littermates at mealtimes.

Do not show any signs of anxiety by trying to coax him to eat, or overfeed him by giving him extra food because he cleaned his bowl so fast. He will soon get used to eating alone as he settles into his new routine.

The first night

The first few nights in a new home can be very distressing for a puppy. He has never been alone before and the routine he has lived by and accepted is gone.

There are different views about where the puppy should sleep. Some people advise that the puppy should be left in his bed or crate in the designated area, ignoring all crying and howling, to prevent bad nighttime habits.

However, I believe this causes too much stress and anxiety to the puppy. The puppy will settle at night much quicker if he gets used to separation from the family gradually.

If you have a crate for your puppy, put it in your bedroom and let the puppy sleep in it for the first few nights. A quiet word and your presence will reassure the puppy. Line the crate with plenty of paper and some cozy bedding at one end.

After a few days you will find that the puppy will adapt to his new surroundings. Then he should be confident enough to sleep on his own at night.

Your puppy may be slightly unsettled for a few days as he adjusts to his new nighttime routine, but he should cope without it causing

him too much concern. Eventually you will both have the benefit of an undisturbed night.

A rescued dog

It can be very rewarding to give a dog another chance for a happy life, but if you provide a home for a rescued adult or adolescent German Shepherd, he will need patience, kindness, and common sense to help him settle into his new home. It is important to remember that everything will be strange and unfamiliar to your new dog, as he will have been used to different rules, different routines, and different people.

Follow the advice given for a new puppy, allowing your rescued dog a chance to get to know his surroundings and the members of his new family. It may take him a few days or a few weeks to settle in with his new family, during which time he may be slightly subdued.

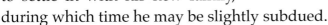

Many owners of rescued dogs say it takes a few months before a dog feels confident enough to show his true personality. Regardless of this, house rules and care plans need to be in place right from the start. A dog will find it much easier to settle in if you are consistent in your handling from the beginning. If your dog understands what is expected of him, he will adapt more easily to the new regime and will soon become an integral member of the family.

Housetraining

New owners often express concern about housetraining their German Shepherd puppy, but this need not be a problem, providing you take the time to follow some practical guidelines.

Your puppy will need to go:

- Immediately after he wakes up.
- Soon after eating or drinking.
- First thing in the morning (no time for you to have a cup of coffee first!).
- After any excitement, such as visitors arriving or the children coming home from school.
- After he has been playing or any stimulating activity.
- If you see him looking agitated, sniffing the ground, or circling around.
- More or less every hour.
- As soon as he is let out of his crate or exercise pen.
- Last thing at night.

Puppies have an instinctive tendency to move away from their sleeping area to go to the toilet; this begins as early as three weeks old. Successful housetraining just develops this instinct.

Puppies do not have much control of their bodily functions, and when they feel the need to relieve themselves, they really cannot hold on. You will need to be vigilant, consistent, and very patient, especially in the first few weeks. Your new puppy will not know what is expected of him, so you must show him what you want. Give him frequent opportunities for toileting in a designated area of the yard or street, and try to avoid mistakes in the house.

You must establish a routine of taking your puppy to the same place outside at the predictable times that he will want to go to the toilet. Luckily, this is quite simple.

You must stay outside with him, and do not become impatient if he does not go right away. Puppies are easily distracted—a leaf or blade of grass blowing in the wind will attract his attention. Give him time to settle down, say your chosen cue word, and praise him as soon as he performs. When you are unable to keep an eye on him, put him in his crate or playpen to restrict him temporarily and avoid housetraining setbacks.

Housetraining tips

When accidents happen

Accidents do happen, and if you see your puppy about to squat, quickly interrupt him—clap your hands or call his name to get his attention. Then encourage him to follow you outside and reward him

for finishing off out of the house. Never be angry with him, hit him, shout at him, or use any other harsh methods if he has an accident in the house. This will only confuse and upset the puppy, causing him to lose confidence in you and hide away instead of letting you know when he wants to go to the toilet.

Choosing a diet

One of the important aspects of daily care is providing your dog with the best nutrition. It is vital for his health and well-being to eat a good-quality, balanced diet.

A good-quality diet must contain essential nutrients, protein, fat, carbohydrates, vitamins, and minerals in sufficient quantities to suit the different stages in his life—from puppyhood to old age. Fresh drinking water must always be available.

Commercial diets

Canned food, semi-moist, pouch, and complete dry food are all convenient to use, but vary in quality depending on the ingredients. Super-premium, complete dog food producers have researched extensively to provide nutritionally balanced diets, especially during the growth phase. It is not necessary to add supplements; in fact, they may even be harmful.

A food that contains the highest quality ingredients is, of course, more expensive. But it will pay off in the health and vitality of your dog.

Raw diets

Raw diets may come fresh or frozen or freeze-dried, or you might choose to prepare your dog's diet yourself. They typically contain raw meat, bones, organ meats, fat, vegetables, and sometimes, some cooked grains. Proponents of raw diets believe they are providing the dog with a food that is very close to the natural diet if she would eat in the wild.

If you're buying a raw diet, look for a statement on the label that says it's complete and balanced. If you want to prepare the diet yourself, work with a veterinary nutritionist to formulate a healthy diet for your dog. There are a lot of raw diet recipes on the Internet, but recent research has found that the majority of them do not offer complete and balanced nutrition.

Feeding schedule

Puppies have little stomachs and their digestive system is very sensitive, so you need to feed a high-quality, digestible food that is specially formulated for puppies. Your puppy will need four meals a day until he is around 12 weeks old; at this stage he can be fed three meals a day. From about six months, feed him twice a day.

If you are feeding a commercial food, follow the product's instructions and divide the daily ration by the number of meals you are feeding per day. It is import-ant to remember that the feeding amounts given are a guide, and your puppy may need more or less, depend-ing on his activity level.

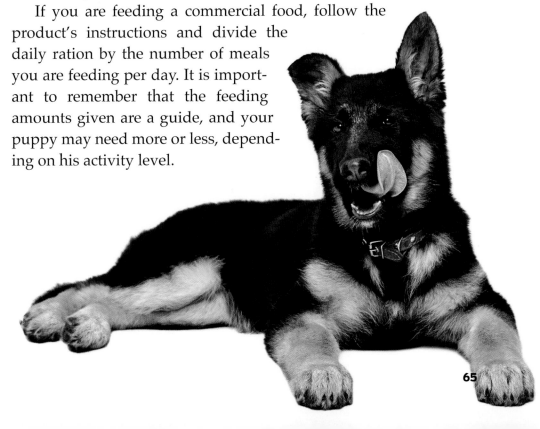

Establish a routine that is convenient for you and try to feed your dog at the same time and place every day. He should be allowed to eat in peace and not be disturbed by people coming and going, or children playing near his bowl. If you have another dog, do not leave them unattended when they are being fed.

Bones and chews

To help relieve the discomfort of teething, I give my puppies large marrow bones to gnaw. It helps with the removal of loose puppy teeth, and, at the same time, all the chewing works the jaw muscles, which appears to help the ears come up.

I do not give bones to our adult German Shepherds, even though I know they would enjoy them. With their powerful jaws they would eat the bones rather than just chew on them, which could cause severe constipation. Some bones, such as turkey, pork, and cooked chicken, should never be given to dogs as they splinter easily, causing intestinal blockage or cuts to the throat.

Rawhide chews are very popular, but a German Shepherd will quickly reduce them to a soft mush and try to swallow large pieces. Dogs have been known to choke to death on these. If you give bones or chews to your dog, always supervise him.

Ideal weight

Calculating the amount of food your German Shepherd will need daily to keep him fit and healthy will depend on his age, activity level, and the environment he lives in. It is important to watch his weight. As a general guide, you should be able to feel his ribs but not see them.

Not providing enough food, or feeding a diet with a poor nutritional level, will result in an underweight dog whose ribs are very visible and whose coat is dull and scruffy.

Dangers of obesity

The idea that the overfed, fat, roly-poly puppy will make a bigger adult is mistaken. The accelerated growth and strain on the body could lead to serious malformations of the joints and bones. Keep your puppy at a good body weight, and let him grow up in his own time.

Unfortunately, obesity in adult dogs is becoming widespread, and with it comes an increase in weight-related medical problems. A high body fat percentage increases anesthetic and surgical risks. With increased body weight, there is more physical stress placed on the muscles, bones and joints, and this can result in severe arthritis and joint problems in later life. Increased amounts of fat are also deposited around the internal organs, as in humans, and result in reduced function or dysfunction. Obesity can be a contributor to other health issues, such as diabetes, heart disease, and breathing problems.

Remember that you are responsible for your Shepherd's health and well-being, and by over-feeding you are literally killing your dog with misplaced kindness.

Chapter 6

Caring for Your German Shepherd

The German Shepherd is a relatively easy breed to care for, but it is important to keep a close eye on your dog, noting any changes—no matter how minor they appear to be. If you spot any problems early on, the chances of a successful outcome are greatly increased.

Grooming

The German Shepherd has a double coat, made up of a dense undercoat and harsh-textured outer coat. She will need regular grooming to remove dead hair and to make sure the coat stays in good condition. During the change of seasons, she sheds a large amount of hair, so daily grooming using your undercoat rake will keep her looking tidy and will keep tufts of her fur from coming out all over the carpet—or anything else she brushes up against.

Long-coated German Shepherds are higher maintenance and will

require almost daily brushing and combing to stop the coat from tangling and forming mats. To prevent a dull or dusty appearance to the coat, wipe your dog all over with a velvet cloth or grooming glove.

It is a good idea to get your German Shepherd puppy used to being groomed. Choose a time when she is not too lively and playful. Brush her daily for just a short time, using a soft brush. Use gentle strokes from the head to the tail, and reward her for cooperating. She will soon get used to the procedure.

Bathing

Frequent bathing is not recommended, as this will strip the coat of its natural oils. If the coat is really dirty, or after a heavy shed, a bath using a gentle dog shampoo may be needed. Make sure the water is not too hot or too cold, and avoid getting shampoo or water in your dog's eyes and ears. In general, a healthy puppy should not need bathing.

Teeth

You will need to be very gentle when you examine your puppy's mouth, because while she is teething, her gums will be sore. They may also be red and swollen. If a baby canine tooth remains in place as the permanent canine comes through, it can force the canine tooth to erupt farther forward than normal; it will also leave the puppy with two sets of teeth. Consult your veterinarian, as the baby canines may need removing.

Dogs build up tartar on their teeth, which can result in tooth decay and gum disease. Get your dog used to having her teeth cleaned from an early age, using a special dog toothpaste and soft brush.

Ears

Check the ears are clean; ear cleaners are available from the vet for routine use. Do not use cotton swabs, as you risk probing too deeply into the ear canal. Watch out for signs of redness, brown discharge, or a bad smell, which may be the start of a problem. Questions? Ask your vet.

Nails

It is a good idea to accustom your puppy to having her paws touched. Gently hold each paw, look at her nails, and reward her with a small treat. This will help when you need to trim her nails.

If the nails have grown too long, you will need to trim the tip of each nail, using guillotine-type nail clippers. Trimming little and often is best, to avoid cutting the quick, which is the soft inner part that contains nerves and blood vessels. This is difficult to see in a German Shepherd's dark nails but, if accidentally cut, it will bleed and will be painful for the dog. If you are unsure about trimming your dog's nails, ask your vet or the dog's breeder to help.

Socialization

Every time you take your German Shepherd out, you are representing all of the breed. It is not difficult to raise your dog to be confident and sociable, but there are two contributing factors that will affect the outcome: the puppy's inherited traits and her life experiences.

You cannot alter her genetic make-up, but you can have a tremendous influence on her life experiences. Hopefully, the breeder has produced the correct character by selecting the parents for their temperament as well as health and looks; this is the first important foundation for your puppy.

The home environment

Many of our household items can appear frightening to a small puppy. It is very important to accustom your puppy gradually to the sights and sounds of the television, the vacuum cleaner, and the washing machine in a calm, controlled way. Care must be taken not to startle the puppy as she is habituating to your domestic environment.

Similarly, when you take your puppy out the first few times, keep away from busy roads with cars and trucks speeding past; even bicycles can be a very frightening experience for a vulnerable puppy. A bad experience can set up a lifetime fear.

I find taking a puppy to a parking lot, where vehicles are moving slowly, and playing with her at a distance from them, allows her to see and hear what is going on around her without feeling apprehensive or overwhelmed. It is also a great place for the puppy to see and meet people. Some will be in a hurry, and some may come and say hello to your puppy, so make sure you have some tasty treats to feed her as she meets someone new, so the experience is a rewarding one.

Socializing with other dogs

Dogs come in all shapes and sizes, and for your puppy to be sociable around other dogs, she will benefit from meeting a variety of adult dogs with good social skills who are used to interacting with unfamiliar puppies.

Puppies need to learn how to communicate with

other dogs, as often their social skills are clumsy and extreme during dog-to-dog greetings. Great care must be taken that unfamiliar dogs do not frighten your puppy when you are in a public place. You must protect her from encounters with other dogs unless you are absolutely sure they will do her no harm.

Early encounters

The earlier a puppy has enjoyable encounters with things she will come into contact with later in life, the more sociable and well-balanced an adult she will grow into, and the less prone to developing problem behaviors. As time goes on, new experiences will be viewed as normal—not strange or scary—as long as the puppy has been given positive exposure to as much as possible before 12 weeks old.

Do not make the mistake of thinking that because your eight-week-old German Shepherd puppy is friendly and playful, you do not need to start socializing her yet. If you miss the early, important weeks, she will have difficulty developing her social skills.

Socializing is an exciting time as you help your puppy to discover something new every day, with your support and encouragement. Let her familiarize herself with new experiences at her own pace; allow her to approach, investigate, and even retreat if she is not quite sure of something. Do not overwhelm her; her natural curiosity will bring her forward to investigate, and then she can be rewarded.

Do not try to verbally reassure or soothe any fearful behavior. The puppy will interpret this as a reward for her behavior, and you will be unintentionally training her to become fearful. Instead, do not show any concern; encourage her, and use play to distract her and reduce her apprehension. If she seems fearful in many different situations and is unable to recover from quickly, ask your veterinarian to recommend a behavioral trainer to help you.

The older German Shepherd

Many German Shepherds are quite active well into their veteran years. Even so, it is wise to make some changes to your dog's care. Adjusting her diet to a specially formulated food for seniors will

help prevent some age-related problems, such as obesity and constipation, and will be much easier for her to digest. A raised feeding bowl can make it easier for her, especially if arthritis is becoming a problem. You should also ensure she has comfortable, soft bedding to rest on.

The older German Shepherd will find it easier to cope with two or three shorter walks rather than one long walk. Watcher her water intake, and note any signs of coughing, limping, or changes in behavior. Talk to your vet, who may suggest treatment to keep her more mobile and comfortable.

There are many treatments your vet can offer for age-related diseases, but there may come a time when an incurable illness or physical deterioration means your dog's quality of life has reached an unacceptable level. Making the decision to let her go is almost unbearable after sharing your life for so long with your faithful friend, but you must do what is best for your dog. Stay with her, stroking and talking to her as she slips away peacefully, and take comfort knowing you have taken care of your beloved pet's welfare to the very end.

Chapter 7

Training Your German Shepherd

Training connects you with your dog as you discover the sheer joy of communicating and tuning into your dog's needs. People wrongly say they do not need to train their dog because he is "only a pet." Training is about teaching your dog to be reliable when you take him out; he will travel well and be a well-behaved companion as he accompanies you to school, to shops, and on family outings. A German Shepherd enjoys learning new activities, and with positive training methods, you will stimulate his active mind.

How dogs learn

The vast majority of your dog's behavior is the result of reinforcement. This term covers basically anything your dog likes: food, playing, toys, tone of voice, petting, access to the outside, access to a certain person—and one most people do not consider, escaping from something unpleasant.

When training your German Shepherd, the reinforcement procedure should be as follows: your dog does something you like, so you immediately do something your dog likes. This is a very powerful and fast method of training, because if an action brings reward and pleasure, the dog will almost certainly do it again. If an action brings something unpleasant or nothing at all, the dog is less likely to do it again.

For the dog to associate his actions with the consequences, timing is crucial. The consequences must be immediate because, unlike people, dogs do not have the ability to reason that something that happened earlier can result in something good or bad happening to them later.

Training guidelines

Using positive motivation and reward training methods will produce a happy, cooperative dog. A German Shepherd is highly intelligent and capable of learning quickly.

Regardless of whether he is a puppy or an adult, training will always be more successful if you take the time to do a little research into developing and improving your handling skills. There are a few important guidelines that will enhance your ability to train your German Shepherd.

Evaluate the dog

Before every training session, check that he is healthy, has been exercised (to relieve himself), and has not just been fed a big meal. Be aware of his temperament, drives, training experience, or if there are any environmental or behavioral issues.

Be prepared

Evaluate yourself honestly, including assessing your physical and emotional state at each training session. Be flexible and ready to adapt training techniques to suit your dog or situation at any time. Know your own limitations. Respect the dog as a living, feeling individual. Understand the dog's body language and signals. Never train when you are angry.

Be aware of the environment

Make sure the environment is likely to promote successful training. When teaching new commands, begin your dog's training without distractions, as these may compete for the dog's attention. Factors that can affect the dog should be taken into consideration, such as people and animal distractions, weather conditions, surrounding noise, and ground surface. Learn to anticipate distractions.

Get ready

Make sure the appropriate equipment for your training is readily accessible, including toys or food for reward, and a correctly fitted collar and leash. Use all equipment correctly and humanely.

Have a training plan

Draw up a clear plan for each training session, and be consistent with verbal cues and any visual signals you intend to use. Decide how you are going to pronounce the sound and tone of each cue and consistently say each cue in its own unique way every time it is used.

Break it down

Help the dog to understand what is required by breaking down the behavior you are training into small, clear, progressive steps. Make sure the dog is successful and confident at each step before moving on to the next. Continually evaluate the dog's reaction and be aware of its meaning.

Be adaptable, and if the dog is showing confusion or continually making errors, be prepared to back up to a level at which the dog was successful. Break the required behavior into concepts the dog can understand. Be clear with verbal cues and hand signals. Let the dog relax while you think about the problem and come up with a solution.

Establish reliability

Gradually build the dog's understanding of each cue. The dog should respond correctly without hesitation before you add distractions, or increase distance or duration. Only change or add one element at a time. Dogs are context-specific learners and do not generalize easily. This means they may have problems responding to training in a different environment, for example.

Correct training strategy ensures reliability—everywhere, every time, no matter what is happening. Sometimes return to an easier level to build confidence, but always reward the dog for responding correctly. He will learn incrementally advancing skills during each training session, and will respond reliably as increasingly challenging distractions are added.

Find motivation

Find out what your dog finds rewarding and use it. It might be food, a toy, a ball, or praise. Most dogs like a variety of rewards, so use different ones to keep the dog interested and trying to win his favorite.

Release words at the end of a skill (such as "okay" or "finished") release the dog to indulge in a behavior he wants and can be an excellent reward. Between or during formal exercises this gives the dog an enthusiastic release to interact and engage in play with you.

Know when to stop

A training session should end on a success that the dog is well rewarded for. However, you should remain flexible to change your overall training plan if the environment or circumstances change in a way that could adversely affect you or the dog. It is better to end or interrupt a training session as soon as you feel it is detrimental to successful learning for the dog, so that you can finish on a positive note.

With gradual and thorough training, patience and a calm attitude, doing your best to ensure all components are in place, you will set your dog up for success.

Mixed messages

Processing the meaning of words is not a natural behavior for a dog. The word has to be consistently associated with the action it is intended to cue, and then rewarded, for the dog to learn the meaning. Each word must have one meaning: for example, "Down" means lie down. It should not be used if you want the dog to stop jumping up.

Dogs are very sensitive to the tone and pitch of your voice, so when you have decided which words all the family will be using for cues, the tone of voice must also be consistent. It will be easier for the dog to associate the word with his actions if he hears it while he is displaying the behavior.

First lessons

It is never too soon to start training. In fact, you can start almost as soon as your puppy has settled into his new home.

Wearing a collar

It is a good idea to get your puppy used to wearing a collar. Most puppies find it strange at first, so introduce it gradually. It should be neither too tight, to irritate or hurt, nor too loose, so that it could slip off.

Put the collar on when the puppy is interested in something else—for example, during a play session. He may scratch at it to start with, but if you distract him with a toy or food, he will soon forget about it. Leave the collar on for just 5 to 10 minutes for the first few times.

When the puppy is not supervised, remove the collar so it cannot get caught on something.

Leash training

Begin with a very gentle introduction to the leash when your puppy is happy wearing his collar. As soon as the leash is attached to the collar, encourage the puppy to come to you for a fuss and a treat.

Take a small step and coax the puppy to move forward beside you. If he is reluctant to move, do not tug the leash or drag him; just encourage him again, offering a food treat to lure him forward. As soon as he moves forward, give him lots of praise. This will be enough for the first leash lesson. Repeat over the next few days, practicing in the house and outside. Gradually increase the number of steps your puppy is taking with his leash attached.

Always keep the leash loose, so that he does not get used to pulling you. If the puppy starts to pull, stand still, make an encouraging sound to get his attention, and prompt him to come back to you. Then praise and reward him. Take a step forward when the leash is loose.

Get the puppy's attention on you by using his favorite toy or food held on your left side, just in front and above his nose. Get him to follow for a few paces. Say "Heel" as you reward him. The correct position at your left side, the word "Heel," and the food reward must all happen at the same time for the puppy to understand where you want him to be, and to associate the reward with the behavior. These early lessons will imprint the idea of walking on a loose leash.

Come when called

Responding to the recall is one of the most valuable exercises you can teach your puppy. If he learns to come back on cue, he will enjoy a better quality of life because you will be able to give him off-leash exercise when it is safe to do so.

A good recall starts with your relationship with your dog; he must enjoy coming back to you because he finds you the most important and exciting thing in his life. Many owners say their dog always comes back when called, except if there are other dogs, people, or squirrels around. What this actually means is the dog only comes back when he is not interested in something else.

A reliable recall has to be taught. Do not assume that because your eight-week-old puppy happily rushes up to you when you call him, that he knows what "Come" means. Very young puppies are naturally inclined to stay close and come when called. Unless you reward the puppy for coming with praise, a treat, or even a game with a toy every time he comes, the cue "Come" will have no meaning.

Unless you are certain your dog will come away from distractions, keep him on a long training line (approx. 33 feet /10 meters long) to make sure he responds to your recall cue. You can let him

 Reliable Recalls

The consequences of behavior—good or bad—is how dogs learn to associate the cue with the desired action. The word "Come" should always mean something pleasurable for your puppy. You should invest a lot of time in teaching a recall.

• Practice calling your puppy in the house and in the yard, encouraging him to come to you. Never grab at him if he runs past you, as it will become a game of keep-away.

• Call your puppy to you often, touch his collar, and give him a treat.

• When you take him out, do not fall into the trap of only calling him back to put on his leash and end his games. It will not take long for an intelligent German Shepherd to ignore the recall cue because it means the end of fun.

• Instead, during an off-leash walk, regularly call him back, reward him, and then send him off again. Sometimes put the leash on, walk a few paces, remove the leash, and play with him.

drag the line or you can hold the end. If he ignores your recall cue, give a little tug on the line, call him in a happy or upbeat tone, and encourage him to come right up to you. Immediately reward his return.

Do not let bad habits develop by allowing your dog to choose not to come when he is called, or punishing him when he does eventually return to you. Practice calling him to you in lots of different places. A good way of building up a strong response to the recall is to ask someone to hold your dog and then call him to you.

Stationary exercises

The "Sit" and "Down" cues are not difficult to teach if you are using positive rewards. Even a very young puppy is capable of understanding. Work on these before progressing to the "Stay" exercise.

Sit: step-by-step

• Hold a treat in front of your puppy's nose, and raise the treat up and very slightly back over his head. As he looks up, he will drop into a Sit. As soon as he sits, reward him.

• Repeat several times, and then introduce the word "Sit" as he drops into position.

• Do the same at mealtimes. Hold his bowl up, tell him to "Sit," and feed him as soon as he does. He will soon automatically sit before being fed.

Down: step-by-step

• Start with your puppy in a Sit. Hold a treat under his nose, place your other hand gently on his shoulders, and slowly lower the treat to the ground between his paws. The treat will lure him into the Down position.

• Keep your hand over the treat until your puppy lies down. Reward by letting him eat the treat on the ground between his paws. This will encourage him to keep his head near the floor rather than follow your hand for the reward.

• Introduce the cue "Down" as he drops to the floor.

As well as luring your puppy into position, you can teach him to associate the word with the action by simply watching for him to sit or lie down naturally, and saying "Sit" or "Down" as he goes into position, and then reward him.

When your puppy is going into these positions on cue, practice getting him to sit or lie down before you give him something he wants—such as a favorite toy, going out the door, or fetching a ball. Practice in many different places.

Stay: step-by-step

Teaching a solid stay takes time and patience. A puppy does not have the necessary self control to stay for very long. A careful introduction to the concept of staying in one place until given a release cue will result in a dog who is confident and reliable to the cue "Stay." Do not start teaching this exercise when your puppy is excited or wanting to play. Wait until he is calm and relaxed.

• Start by teaching him to stay in the Down position, first making sure there are no distractions or anything in the environment that could frighten him.

• With the puppy in the Down, say "Stay" and wait two seconds. Reward him and say your release word, "Okay."

• Repeat a few times, gradually increasing the time before rewarding. Remain close to the puppy, because at this stage you are building up time, not distance. You are positively reinforcing the Down-Stay by rewarding him for remaining in position.

• Sometimes wait four seconds and then say "Stay"; wait another three seconds, reward, then release with "Okay."

• When your puppy will stay down for 10 to 15 seconds, you can begin to add some distance. Tell him "Stay," take a step away, wait five seconds, return, reward, and release.

• Repeat a few times. Then, if all is going well, take three steps away and wait for five seconds. This must be taught slowly. Give

him confidence when he is staying by gently saying "Stay" and "Good boy" to reinforce the position. This will also keep his attention on you.

Stopping unacceptable behavior

There will times when you need to call a halt to unacceptable behavior. This should not be done in anger or frustration. You must react in a calm but firm manner, so your dogs understands exactly what you want from him.

"No" is urgent and should be instantly followed. "Leave" is a cue taught as part of basic good manners.

No: step-by-step

"No" is taught as a counter to unwanted behavior. The behavior must be interrupted and then the dog's attention should be redirected back to you. So, in essence, "No" means "stop what you are doing and look at me." Clearly defined in this way, you and your dog both know what is required and when he has got it right.

• The type of interruption depends on the situation.

• A quick movement toward the dog as you say "No" in a deep, firm voice may be sufficient to stop him.

• You may need to use a loud sound, such as a can with a few pebbles inside, which will make a sharp noise when shaken.

• Whatever you use as an interrupter to stop the behavior must immediately be followed by praise and reward, communicating to the dog that he is now behaving in an acceptable manner.

The key element of correction is surprise, not pain or fear. It should be split-second and instantly effective; it must be given calmly, followed by positive reinforcement when the dog's behavior is correct.

An example of an unwanted behavior that can be stopped using an interrupter is mouthing by a puppy or young dog. Correction should never be used when teaching your dog a new behavior.

Control exercises

These are important lessons, teaching your German Shepherd to respond to your wishes—even when he has something he does not want to give up.

Leave: step-by-step

You cannot expect your puppy to leave something unless he knows what it means.

• Ask your puppy to "Sit," give him a small treat, and then hold another one between your finger and thumb.

• Tell him to "Leave" in a calm voice and close your hand over the treat, keeping your hand still. If your puppy licks or paws your hand, ignore him.

- Only say "Leave" once. Be patient and wait until he moves his head away from your hand and then immediately give him the treat.
- Repeat this several times. Your puppy will soon figure out that he must move his head away when you say "Leave" to get his treat.
- Gradually build the time he has to wait for the treat without jumping on you, before rewarding him.
- Once you can see he understands the word "Leave," use it with other items. As soon as he responds correctly, reward him.

If you want your puppy to relinquish something in his mouth, teach "Leave" for a treat or a more exciting game with a different toy.

- Hold a treat in front of his nose.
- As soon as he loosens his grip on the toy to get the treat, say or "Leave."
- Catch the toy in your hand as you praise him and give him the treat. As soon as he has finished, let him have the toy back to continue the game, as this is also a reward for giving it up on cue.
- Practice in quick, short sessions, and he will soon be happy to follow your cue.

Wait: step-by-step

This exercise is all about self-control; it means your dog should wait calmly until you tell him to do something else. He must wait while a door or gate is opened, wait to go in or out of the car, and wait before a toy is thrown. "Wait" helps the dog to develop self-control. I like my dogs to make eye contact with me before being released from the "Wait" cue.

- Initially, say "Wait" and make a little sound, something like clicking with your tongue.
- As your puppy looks at you to investigate the sound, immediately give him permission to do what he was waiting to do.
- Repeat this in different situations, gradually extending the waiting time before the release.

The ideal owner

There are many attributes I could list to describe the ideal owner of a German Shepherd, including everything previously mentioned about enhancing your training and handling skills. Here are some essentials:

• An ideal owner is consistent and decisive, patient and emotionally disciplined.

• We must be fair in what we expect, teaching our German Shepherds to live in harmony with us out of respect and trust, never fear.

• We must have a sense of humor and appreciate that a dog is just a dog; he has no sense of fair play, and does nothing out of spite.

• Our own anger or life's frustrations must never be taken out on the dog, as this compromises the quality of our relationship with him.

As a training instructor, I have been saddened to see the utter confusion in a dog due to his owner's impatience, harshness, and even punishment because the dog cannot figure out what is wanted. An ideal German Shepherd owner will understand that communication is two-way and will endeavor to give the dog clear instructions in a way he can understand.

Chapter 8

Keeping Your German Shepherd Busy

There are many activities at which a German Shepherd excels and you can enjoy sharing. The mental and physical stimulation of these activities is a challenge she will thrive on.

Canine Good Citizen

The AKC runs the Canine Good Citizen program. It promotes responsible ownership and helps you to train a well-behaved dog who will fit in with the community. The program tests your dog on basic manners, alone and with other people and dogs around. It's excellent for all pet owners and is also an ideal starting point if you plan to compete with your German Shepherd in any sport when she is older.

Agility

Agility is a fast and fun activity; both the handler and dog have to be fit, and your German Shepherd must be under control. To learn to use the equipment you will need to find a club that specializes in the sport. The agility course is a series of obstacles, which includes jumps (upright and long), weaving poles, A-frame, dog walk, see-saw, and tunnels. All of this is done at speed, with the winner completing the course in the fastest time with the fewest faults.

Obedience

Training your dog in formal obedience can range from regularly attending a training club to competing in competitive obedience trials where you progress through the levels from novice to advanced. Exercises include heel work, recall, stays, retrieve, scent discrimination, send-away, and distance control. Competitive obedience requires accuracy and precision.

German Shepherds at dog shows

Tracking

The versatile German Shepherd is a good choice for this demanding sport where the dog must learn to follow scent trails of varying age, over different types of terrain.

Schutzhund

This international sport originated in Germany, with the name deriving from the German word for "protection dog." It is designed to test the Shepherd's mental stability, endurance, ability to scent, courage and willingness to work.

The show ring

If your dog is a good example of the breed and conforms closely to the breed standard, you may be interested in showing.

There are several levels of dog shows, from fun companion shows, where many owners start with their pets, to the most prestigious specialist breed Championship shows, where the German Shepherd will need to be of very high merit to be successful.

Chapter 9

Health Care

We are fortunate that the German Shepherd is a healthy dog, and with good routine care, a well-balanced diet, and sufficient exercise, most dogs will experience few health problems.

However, it is your responsibility to put a program of preventive health care in place—and this should start from the moment your puppy, or adult dog, arrives in his new home.

Parasites

No matter how well you look after your German Shepherd, you will have to accept that parasites—internal and external—are ever present, and you need to take preventive action.

Internal parasites live inside your dog. These are the various worms. Most will find a home in the digestive tract, but there is also a parasite that lives in the heart. If infestation is unchecked, a dog's health will be severely jeopardized, but routine preventive treatment is simple and effective. External parasites live on your dog's body—in his skin and fur, and sometimes in his ears.

Vaccinating Your Dog

Dogs are subject to a number of contagious diseases. In the old days, these were killers, and resulted in heartbreak for many owners. Vaccinations have made the incidence of the major infectious diseases very rare. However, this will only remain the case if all pet owners follow a strict policy of vaccinating their dogs.

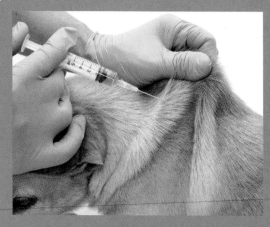

The American Animal Hospital Association and the American Veterinary Medical Association have issued vaccination guidelines that apply to all breeds of dogs. They divide the available vaccines into two groups: core vaccines, which every dog should get, and non-core vaccines, which are optional.

Core vaccines are canine parvovirus-2, distemper, and adenovirus-2. Puppies should get vaccinated every three to four weeks between the ages of 6 and 16 weeks, with the final dose at 14 to 16 weeks of age. If a dog older than 16 weeks is getting their first vaccine, one dose is enough. Dogs who received an initial dose at less than 16 weeks should be given a booster after one year, and then every three years or more thereafter.

Rabies is also a core vaccine. For puppies less than 16 weeks old, a single dose should be given no earlier than 12 weeks of age. Revaccination is recommended annually or every three years, depending on the vaccine used and state and local laws.

Non-core vaccines are canine parainfluenza virus, Bordetella bronchiseptica, canine influenza virus, canine measles, leptospirosis, and Lyme disease. The dog's exposure risk, lifestyle, and geographic location all come into play when deciding which non-core vaccines may be appropriate for your dog. Have a conversation with your veterinarian about the right vaccine protocol for your dog.

Roundworm

This is found in the small intestine. Signs of infestation will be a poor coat, a potbelly, diarrhea, and lethargy. Prospective mothers should be treated before mating, but it is almost inevitable that parasites she may have will be passed on to the puppies. For this reason, a breeder will start a worming program, which you will need to continue. Ask your vet for advice on treatment, which will need to continue throughout your dog's life.

Tapeworm

Infection occurs when the dog ingests fleas or lice. The adult worm takes up residence in the small intestine, releasing mobile segments (which contain eggs), which can be seen in a dog's feces as small rice-like grains. The only other obvious sign of infestation is irritation of the anus. Again, routine preventive treatment is required throughout your dog's life.

Heartworm

This parasite is transmitted by mosquitoes, and is found in all parts of the USA, although its prevalence does vary. Heartworms live in the right side of the heart and larvae can grow up to 14 inches (35 cm) long. A dog with heartworm is at severe risk from heart failure, so preventive treatment, as advised by your vet, is essential. Dogs should also have regular tests to check for the presence of infection.

Lungworm

Lungworm is a parasite that lives in the heart and major blood vessels supplying the lungs. It can cause many problems, such as breathing difficulties, excessive bleeding, sickness, diarrhea, seizures, and even death. The dog becomes infected when ingesting slugs and snails, often accidentally when rummaging through undergrowth. Lungworm is not common, but it is on the increase and a responsible owner should be aware of it. Fortunately, it is easily preventable, and even affected dogs usually make a full recovery if treated early enough. Your vet will be able to advise you on the risks in your area and what form of treatment may be required.

How to Remove a Tick

If you spot a tick on your dog, do not try to pluck it off, as you risk leaving the hard mouth parts embedded in his skin. The best way to remove a tick is to use a fine pair of tweezers, or you can buy a tick remover. Grasp the tick head firmly and then pull the tick straight out from the skin. If you are using a tick remover, check the instructions, as some recommend a circular twist when pulling. When you have removed the tick, clean the area with mild soap and water.

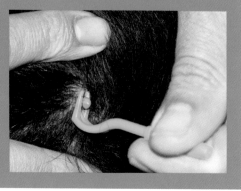

Fleas

A dog may carry many types of fleas. The flea stays on the dog only long enough to feed and breed, but its presence will result in itching. If your dog has an allergy to fleas—usually a reaction to the flea's saliva—she will scratch herself until she is raw. Spot-ons and chewable flea preventives are easy to use and highly effective, and should be given regularly to prevent fleas entirely. Some also prevent ticks.

If your dog has fleas, talk to your veterinarian about the

best treatment. Bear in mind that your entire home, dog's whole environment, and all other pets in your home will also need to be treated.

Ticks

These are blood-sucking parasites that are most frequently found in areas where sheep or deer are present.

The main danger is their ability to pass a wide variety of very serious diseases—including Lyme disease—to both dogs and humans. The preventive you give your dog for fleas generally works for ticks, but you should discuss the best product to use with your veterinarian.

Ear mites

These parasites live in the outer ear canal. The signs of infestation are a brown, waxy discharge, and your dog will often shake her head and scratch her ear.

If you suspect your dog has ear mites, a visit to the vet will be needed so that medicated ear drops can be prescribed.

Cheyletiella mange

These small, white mites are visible to the naked eye and are often referred to as "walking dandruff." They cause a scruffy coat and mild itchiness. They are zoonotic—transferable to humans—so prompt treatment with an insecticide prescribed by your veterinarian is essential.

Chiggers

These are picked up from the undergrowth, and can be seen as bright red, yellow, or orange specks on the webbing between the toes, although this can also be found elsewhere on the body, such as on the ear flaps. Treatment is effective with the appropriate insecticide from your vet.

Skin mites

There are two types of parasite that burrow into a dog's skin. Demodex canis is transferred from a mother to her pups while they are feeding. Treatment is with a topical preparation, and sometimes antibiotics are needed. Refer to your vet.

The other skin mite is sarcoptes scabiei, which causes intense itching and hair loss. It is highly contagious, so all dogs in a household will need to be treated, which involves repeated bathing with a medicated shampoo.

How to Detect Fleas

You may suspect your dog has fleas, but how can you be sure? There are two methods to try.

Run a fine comb through your dog's coat, and see if you can detect the presence of fleas on the skin, or clinging to the comb. Alternatively, sit your dog on some white paper and rub his back. This will dislodge feces from the fleas, which will be visible as small brown specks. To double check, shake the specks on to some damp cotton balls. Flea feces consists of the dried blood taken from the host, so if the specks turn a lighter shade of red, you know your dog has fleas.

Common ailments

As with all living animals, dogs can be affected by a variety of ailments, most of which can be treated effectively after consulting with your vet, who will prescribe appropriate medication and will advise you on how to care for your dog's needs.

Here are some of the more common problems that could affect your German Shepherd, with advice on how to deal with them.

Anal glands

These are two small sacs on either side of the anus, which produce a dark-brown secretion that dogs use when they mark their territory. The anal glands should empty every time a dog defecates, but

if they become blocked or impacted, a dog will experience increasing discomfort. He may nibble at his rear end, or scoot his bottom along the ground to relieve the irritation.

Treatment involves a trip to the vet, who will empty the glands manually. It is important to do this without delay or they could become infected.

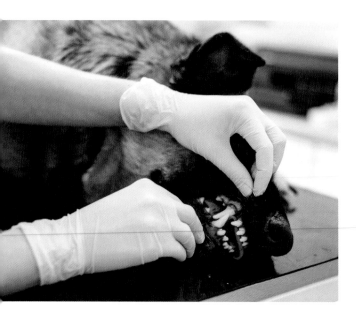

Dental problems

Good dental hygiene will do much to minimize problems with gum infection and tooth decay. If tartar accumulates to the extent that you cannot remove it by brushing, your dog will need to be anesthetized for a dental cleaning by the veterinarian.

Diarrhea

There are many reasons why a dog has diarrhea, but most commonly it is the result of scavenging, a sudden change of diet, or an adverse reaction to a particular type of food.

If your dog is suffering from diarrhea, the first step is to withhold food for a day. It is important that she does not become dehydrated, so make sure that fresh drinking water is available. However, drinking too much can increase the diarrhea, which may be accompanied with vomiting, so limit how much she drinks at any one time.

After allowing the stomach to rest, feed a bland diet, such as white fish or chicken with boiled rice for a few days. In most cases, your dog's motions will return to normal and you can resume normal feeding, although this should be done gradually.

However, if this fails to work and the diarrhea persists for more than a few days, you should consult your vet. Your dog may have an infection, which needs to be treated with antibiotics, or the diarrhea may indicate some other problem that needs expert diagnosis.

Ear problems

The German Shepherd has erect ears, which allow air to circulate, thus reducing the risk of ear infections.

A healthy ear is clean with no sign of redness or inflammation, and no evidence of a waxy brown discharge or a foul odor. If you see your dog scratching his ear, shaking his head, or holding one ear at an odd angle, you will need to consult your vet.

The most likely causes are ear mites, an infection, or there may a foreign body, such as a grass seed, trapped in the ear.

Depending on the cause, treatment is with medicated eardrops, possibly containing antibiotics. If a foreign body is suspected, the vet will need to carry out further investigations.

Eye problems

If your German Shepherd's eyes look red and sore, he may be suffering from conjunctivitis. This may, or may not be accompanied with a watery or a crusty discharge.

Conjunctivitis can be caused by a bacterial or viral infection, it could be the result of an injury, or it could be an adverse reaction to pollen. You will need to consult your vet for a correct diagnosis, but in the case of an infection, treatment with medicated eye drops is effective.

Foreign bodies

Puppies—and some older dogs—cannot resist chewing anything that looks interesting. The toys you choose for your dog should be suitably robust to withstand damage, but children's toys can be irresistible. Some dogs will chew—and swallow—anything from socks, underwear, and other items from the laundry basket, to golf balls and stones from the garden. Obviously, these items are indigestible and could cause an obstruction in your dog's intestine, which is potentially lethal.

The signs to look for are vomiting, and a tucked-up posture. The dog will often be restless and will look as though he is in pain. In this situation, you must get your dog to the vet without delay as surgery will be needed to remove the obstruction.

The other type of foreign body that may cause problems is grass seed. A grass seed can enter an orifice such as a nostril, down an ear, the gap between the eye and the eyelid, or penetrate the soft skin between the toes. It can also be swallowed.

The introduction of a foreign body induces a variety of symptoms, depending on the point of entry and where it travels to. The signs to look for include head shaking, ear scratching, the eruption of an abscess, sore or inflamed eyes, or a persistent cough. The vet will be able to make a proper diagnosis, and surgery may be required.

Lameness or limping

There are a wide variety of reasons why a dog can go lame, from a simple muscle strain to a fracture, ligament damage, or more complex problems with the joints. It takes an expert to make a correct diagnosis, so if you are concerned about your dog, do not delay in seeking help.

The German Shepherd is prone to a number of breed-specific conditions that result in lameness (they're to be discussed later in this chapter), so extra vigilance is required, and care should be taken not to over-exercise a growing dog.

As your German Shepherd becomes elderly, he may suffer from arthritis, which you will see as general stiffness, particularly when he gets up after resting. It will help if you ensure his bed is in a warm, draft-free location, and, if your Shepherd gets wet after exercise, you must dry him thoroughly.

If your Shepherd seems to be in pain, consult your vet, who will be able to help with pain relief medication and nutritional supplements.

Heatstroke

This is a condition that can affect a dog literally within minutes. The greatest danger is if a dog is confined in a car. The temperature can rise dramatically—even on a cloudy day—and unless you are able to lower your dog's temperature, it can be fatal.

The signs of heatstroke include heavy panting and difficulty breathing, bright red tongue and mucous membranes, thick saliva, and vomiting. Eventually, the dog becomes progressively unsteady and passes out.

If your dog appears to be suffering from heatstroke, this is a true emergency. Lie her flat and then cool her as quickly as possible by hosing her or covering her with wet towels. As soon as she has made some recovery, take her to the vet.

Skin problems

If your dog is scratching or nibbling at his skin, the first thing to check for is fleas. There are other parasites that cause itching and hair loss, but you will need a vet to help you find the culprit.

An allergic reaction is another major cause of skin problems. It can be quite an undertaking to find the cause of the allergy, and you will need to follow your vet's advice.

Inherited and breed-disposed disorders

The German Shepherd does have some breed-related disorders. If your dog is diagnosed with any of the diseases listed here, it is important to remember that they can affect offspring, so it is not wise to breed affected dogs.

There are now recognized screening tests that enable breeders to check for carrier and affected individuals, and hence reduce the prevalence of these diseases within the breed. DNA testing is also becoming more widely available, and as research into genetic diseases progresses, more DNA tests are being developed.

Anal furunculosis

This is a very painful disease of the tissues around the anus. There could be a genetic factor. The first sign is the dog constantly licking around the anal area; on inspection, small oozing sores can be seen around the anus. These will have already become deep, painful fistulas and it may be difficult to examine the dog due to the pain.

Veterinary treatment includes antibiotic therapy and surgical removal of all the infected tissue. If this condition is caught early, treatment may be more successful. It seems to develop in middle-aged dogs. German Shepherd owners need to check under the dog's tail regularly to make sure the anal area is clear.

Degenerative myelopathy (DM)

DM is a degenerative neurological disease seen primarily in German Shepherds over five years old. Clinical signs can begin as dragging toes and scuffing nails and progress to rear spinal and hind limb weakness, which may either wane or steadily worsen.

There is no cure, but dietary supplements, controlled exercise, and supportive carts have all been used to help enable a good quality of life. There is a DNA test available to prevent future generations from being affected.

Elbow dysplasia

This is a developmental disease where the elbow does not mature correctly. Signs of lameness are usually seen in younger, large breed dogs. It can affect one or both elbows, and covers several different types of conditions, which can present in one or more of the following ways.

Ununited anconeal process usually develops between the ages of five to seven months, when a fragment of bone of the joint does not unite with the ulna during growth. It is first noticed as foreleg lameness. Fragmented medial coronoid process (FMCP) is when a small piece of bone lies loose in the joint, causing pain and lameness.

Osteochondritis dissecans (OCD) and osteochondrosis (OC) are caused when a piece of cartilage becomes partially or fully detached from the growing bone. Usually the elbow or shoulder joint is affected, but the hock joint on the back leg can also develop the problem.

X-rays are submitted to the Orthopedic Foundation for Animals to assess the soundness of a dog's elbows. Severely affected dogs should not be used for breeding.

Surgery may be needed to correct the abnormalities, but the affected joints will be more prone to arthritis later in life.

Epilepsy

This is an inherited condition in German Shepherds, often first seen as seizures occurring in the younger or middle-aged dog. Treatment is usually in the form of lifelong anticonvulsant medication to control the seizures. Each dog needs to be individually monitored to ensure the right level of medication is being used.

Exocrine pancreatic insufficiency

This condition has a hereditary basis, and has a higher prevalence in the German Shepherd. EPI is an inadequate production of digestive enzymes, resulting in malabsorption, especially of fats, and chronic diarrhea, which is gray and foul-smelling. Despite a ravenous appetite, weight loss will be extreme. A simple blood test will confirm the diagnosis.

Dogs can show a good response to treatment and live a fairly normal life, but affected dogs should not be used for breeding.

Eye disorders

Multifocal retinal dysplasia is the abnormal development of the retina. The mildest form has minimal effect on vision, but severe forms may manifest as complete retinal detachment and blindness. Retinal dysplasia is identified by an eye examination by the Companion Animal Eye Registry (CAER) .

German Shepherds can suffer from hereditary cataracts, where the lens is often affected in younger dogs but may not be evident until later in life. There are varying degrees of severity. The inherited form usually has little effect on eyesight, but if necessary, surgery is usually successful. Screening is available through CAER, which recommends annual eye testing.

Gastric dilatation/volvulus

This condition, commonly known as bloat or gastric torsion, is occurs when the stomach swells visibly (dilatation) and then rotates (volvulus), so that the exit into the small intestine becomes blocked, preventing food from leaving. This results in stomach pain and a bloated abdomen. It is a severe, life-threatening condition that requires immediate veterinary attention (usually surgery) to decompress and return the stomach to its normal position.

There appears to be several risk factors, and by taking the following precautions, you can reduce the risk.

- Feed two or more smaller meals per day.
- Do not allow the dog to drink a large volume of water at one time.
- Do not feed immediately before or after strenuous exercise—wait at least two hours.

Hemophilia A

This is a blood-clotting defect that affects males; females can be carriers but are not affected. It is an inherited disorder where there is a deficiency in Factor VIII, one of the factors involved in the clotting process. This results in bleeding with any traumatic incident, which, if severe, can be life-threatening. There are blood tests available to detect carriers, to help prevent the disease affecting future generations.

Hip dysplasia

Perhaps the most well-known health issue in the breed is hip dysplasia. This is any abnormality of one or both hip joints. In dogs with this structural problem, the ball and socket joint of the hip develops incorrectly so that the head of the femur (ball) and the acetabulum of the pelvis (socket) do not fit snugly. This causes pain in the joint, and may be seen as lameness in dogs as young as five months old, with deterioration into severe arthritis over time.

In severe cases, the dog shows considerable pain, stiffness when getting up, lameness and has difficulty walking. Mildly affected dogs may show no signs and lead a normal life, but arthritis of the joints may develop in later life.

Gentle exercise, keeping the dog at a good weight, anti-inflammatory drugs, and home management are all part of the treatment. Severe cases may require surgery.

Hip dysplasia is thought to have a genetic component, but the mode of inheritance has not been established, since multiple genes are involved. Environmental effects during the rapid growth phase of a young dog, such as over-exercise, excessive weight, and poor nutrition, can also contribute to its development.

All potential breeding animals should be screened by having their hips scored. X-rays are submitted to the Orthopedic Foundation for Animals or PennHIP, where they are graded according to the degree of hip laxity.

Juvenile renal dysplasia

This is a hereditary disease found in the German Shepherd, causing incorrect development of the kidneys, and, in severe cases, renal failure in young dogs. If only mildly affected, there may be no obvious clinical signs, and these carriers have the potential to pass on the defect to future generations. There is no treatment, but a DNA test is available to identify affected individuals and prevent the disease from occurring in future generations.

Panosteitis

This is a cause of sudden, severe lameness, which can alternate from one leg to another. The exact cause of panosteitis is unknown, but dogs often have a high fever at the same time and a virus is suspected. The disease will usually resolve with time, but if signs are severe, then rest and anti-inflammatories may be prescribed.

Pituitary dwarfism

In this condition, the German Shepherd puppy suffers from a failure to produce enough growth hormone, which will result in stunted growth, although the dog does stay in proportion. This inherited condition also results in a woolly, puppy-like coat, which is easily lost, and dark skin on the hairless areas. Often, affected individuals suffer from a shortened life span despite medication.

A DNA test is available to determine genetically affected carriers, to enable breeders to avoid reproducing this disease in future generations.

Von Willebrand's Disease

This disease is characterized by a deficiency in von Willebrand's factor (vWF), which is vital to help platelets form clots and stop bleeding.

There are three types of disease—I, II, and III—with a corresponding increase in severity with increasing number. German Shepherds are most commonly affected by type I, where there is less than 50 percent of the normal amount of vWF. This condition is widespread in the breed, and is also associated with the Doberman Pinscher.

Summing up

This has been a long list of health problems, but it was not my intention to scare you. Acquiring some basic knowledge is an asset, as it will allow you to spot signs of trouble at an early stage. Early diagnosis very often leads to the most effective treatment.

It is wise, when choosing your German Shepherd, to be aware of the potential problems and to ensure that the parent dogs have already been tested for the most severe and prevalent diseases, thereby reducing the likelihood that they will afflict your dog.

The German Shepherd as a breed is a healthy, energetic dog with a zest for life, and annual check-ups will be all he needs. As a companion, he will bring many happy memories in the years you will spend together.

Find Out More

Books

Bradshaw, John, *Dog Sense: How the New Science of Dog Behavior Can Make You a Better Friend to Your Pet*. New York: Basic Books, 2014.

Eldredge, Debra M., DVM, Liisa D. Carlson, DVM, Delbert G. Carlson, DVM, and James M. Giffin, MD, D*og Owner's Home Veterinary Handbook*, 4th Edition. New York: Howell Book House, 2007.

Gerritsen, Resi, and Ruud Haak, *K9 Schutzhund Training: A Manual for IPO Training Through Positive Reinforcement*, 2nd Edition. Edmonton, AL: Dog Training Press, 2014.

Stilwell, Victoria, *Train Your Dog Positively: Understand Your Dog and Solve Common Behavior Problems Including Separation Anxiety, Excessive Barking, Aggression, Housetraining, Leash Pulling, and More!* Berkeley: Ten Speed Press, 2013.

Websites

www.akc.org American Kennel Club

gsdca.org German Shepherd Dog Club of America

www.petmd.com PetMD

www.ukcdogs.com United Kennel Club

www.germanshepherddog.com United Schutzhund Clubs of America

Series Glossary of Key Terms

agility in this case, a canine sport in which dogs navigate an obstacle course

breed standard a detailed written description of the ideal type, size, shape, colors, movement, and temperament of a dog breed

conforms aligns with, agrees with

docked cut or shortened

dysplasia a structural problem with the joints, when the bones do not fit properly together

heatstroke a medical condition in which the body overheats to a dangerous degree

muzzle (n) the nose and mouth of a dog; (v) to place a restraint on the mouth of a dog

neuter to make a male dog unable to create puppies

parasites organisms that live and feed on a host organism

pedigree the formal record of an animal's descent, usually showing it to be purebred

socialization the process of introducing a dog to as many different sights, sounds, animals, people and experiences as possible, so he will feel comfortable with them all

spay to make a female dog unable to create puppies

temperament the basic nature of an animal, especially as it affects their behavior

Index